BALTIMORE RAVENS

THE HISTORY OF THE

Published by Creative Education
123 South Broad Street
Mankato, Minnesota 56001
Creative Education is an imprint of The Creative Company.

DESIGN AND PRODUCTION BY **EVANSDAY DESIGN**

LIBRARY OF CONGRESS CATALOGING-IN-PUBLICATION DATA

Nichols, John, 1966–
The history of the Baltimore Ravens / by John Nichols.
p. cm. — (NFL today)
ISBN 1-58341-288-3
1. Baltimore Ravens (Football team)—History—Juvenile literature.
[1. Baltimore Ravens (Football team)—History. 2. Football—History.]
I. Title. II. Series.

GV956.B3N53 2004
796.332'64'097526—dc22   2003064637

First edition

9 8 7 6 5 4 3 2 1

COVER PHOTO: linebacker Ray Lewis

RAVENS

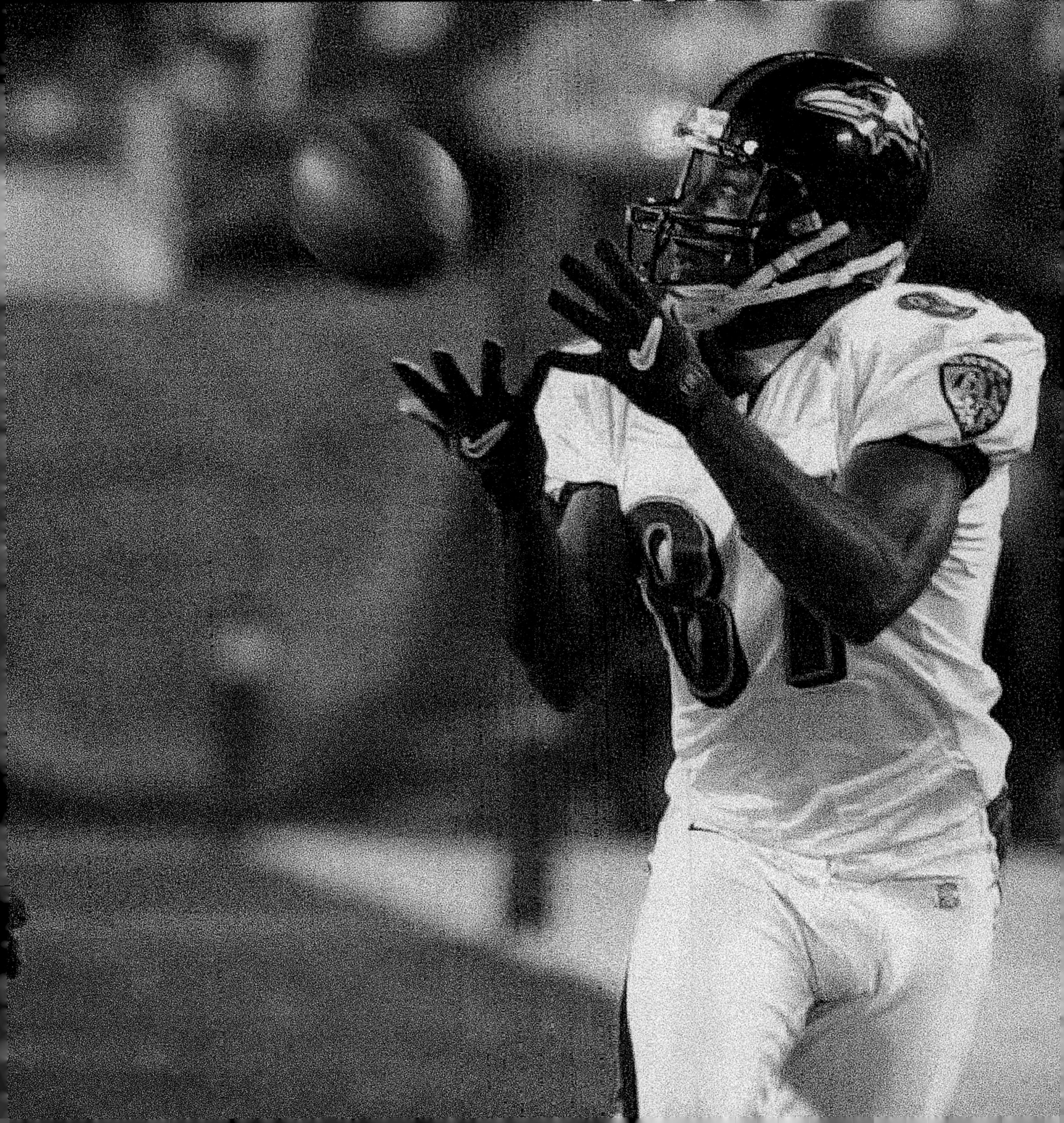

BALTIMORE, MARYLAND, IS ONE OF THE BUSIEST SEAPORTS IN THE UNITED STATES. LOCATED ON BEAUTIFUL CHESAPEAKE BAY, THE CITY HAS BEEN A PROMINENT COMMERCIAL CENTER SINCE COLONIAL TIMES. ONE OF THE CITY'S FINEST MOMENTS CAME IN 1814, WHEN U.S. SOLDIERS BRAVELY DEFENDED BALTIMORE'S FORT McHENRY AGAINST A FIERCE BRITISH NAVAL BARRAGE. THIS BATTLE INSPIRED FRANCIS SCOTT KEY TO COMPOSE THE "STAR-SPANGLED BANNER," THE UNITED STATES' NATIONAL ANTHEM. ANOTHER PART OF BALTIMORE'S RICH HISTORY INVOLVES PROFESSIONAL FOOTBALL. FROM 1953 UNTIL 1983, THE CITY'S SPORTS FANS CHEERED FOR THE BALTIMORE COLTS OF THE NATIONAL FOOTBALL LEAGUE (NFL). BUT DESPITE GREAT SUCCESS AND SUPPORT, THE COLTS MOVED TO INDIANAPOLIS IN 1984. BALTIMORE FANS WERE HEARTBROKEN, BUT IN 1995, THE NFL RETURNED TO BALTIMORE WHEN THE CLEVELAND BROWNS ANNOUNCED THAT THEY WOULD MOVE AND BECOME THE BALTIMORE RAVENS.

[Cornerback Chris McAlister]

THE RAVENS ARE HATCHED>

THE CLEVELAND BROWNS had been a member of the

NFL since 1950, but by the early 1990s, team owner Art

Modell had decided his team could no longer compete fi-

nancially playing in aging Cleveland Municipal Stadium.

In 1996, after the city of Cleveland refused to build a

new home for the Browns, Modell moved his team to

Baltimore, where a new stadium would be built. In mov-

ing to Baltimore, Modell agreed to let Cleveland keep the

Browns name, colors, and records. "I wanted the fans in

Needing a new name, the team conducted a public poll. In the end, it was decided that Maryland's new football team would be called the Ravens. A raven is a large black bird that often appears purple in the sunlight. One of Baltimore's most famous citizens, author Edgar Allen Poe, portrayed a talking raven as the title character in "The Raven," one of his best-known poems.

The Ravens' first step was to hire a head coach. They selected a familiar face for the position: Ted Marchibroda, who had coached the old Baltimore Colts from 1975 to 1979. Marchibroda, an enthusiastic leader, was put in charge of turning around a team that had finished just 5–11 in its final season in Cleveland. The veteran coach knew he could count on quarterback Vinny Testaverde to provide solid offensive leadership, and hard-hitting safety Stevon Moore was an anchor around which the defense could be built. Still, Marchibroda knew the Ravens would need an infusion of young talent if they were to be successful.

In the 1996 NFL Draft, the Ravens used their two first-round picks to acquire giant offensive tackle Jonathan Ogden and ferocious middle linebacker Ray Lewis. The 6-foot-8 and 325-pound Ogden was known for his enormous strength, quick feet, and keen understanding of the game. Lewis, who

had played for the powerful University of Miami Hurricanes in college, was a fierce hitter who added a confident swagger to the defense.

The two rookies stepped right into the Ravens' starting lineup and produced immediate results. Lewis made a team-leading 142 tackles his first year, and Ogden provided wall-like protection for Testaverde, who used the time to throw 33 touchdown passes. Yet despite the efforts of their veteran quarterback and dynamic rookies, the Ravens posted a 4–12 record in 1996. "We took our share of lumps this year," said Coach Marchibroda. "But we had a lot of young players do a lot of growing up. We'll get better."

The Ravens jumped to 6–9–1 in 1997 as Lewis and Ogden continued to improve. Lewis posted an amazing 210 tackles, while Ogden dominated opposing defensive linemen, opening big holes for running backs Byron "Bam" Morris and Earnest Byner. Lewis and Ogden's performances turned heads around the league, earning both players a trip to the Pro Bowl. "Ray and Jonathan are two pieces of the puzzle," said Ravens defensive end Rob Burnett. "We just need to find more pieces."

BALTIMORE BUILDS WITH DEFENSE>

THE RAVENS' BIGGEST weakness in their first two seasons was a soft defense. Despite the efforts of Lewis, the team ranked near the bottom of the NFL in points allowed. In the 1997 NFL Draft, the team addressed some of its needs by selecting linebackers Peter Boulware and Jamie Sharper. Boulware and Sharper teamed with Lewis to form the league's youngest and most promising linebacker trio. "Those three guys can all run, hit, and make plays," said Pittsburgh Steelers head coach Bill Cowher.

Baltimore also acquired some veteran talent to go with its young stars. Mammoth defensive tackle Tony "the Goose" Siragusa and safety Rod Woodson both signed on before the 1998 season. Siragusa, whose round body looked more like a truck driver's than a football player's, became an instant fan favorite with his bulldozing playing style and colorful personality. The 33-year-old

Woodson, who had been a seven-time Pro-Bowler with the Pittsburgh Steelers, gave the team veteran leadership in the defensive backfield.

The 1998 season held great promise for the Ravens. After playing its first two seasons at old Memorial Stadium (where the Colts had formerly played), the team moved into a beautiful new stadium. The switch signaled to many fans and players that the days of the old Colts were finally over and that Baltimore was at last a Ravens town. "Playing at Memorial Stadium was great, but it still sort of belonged to the Colts," said Ravens receiver Michael Jackson. "This place is all ours."

The magic of the new stadium did not change the Ravens' fortunes, however. The improved defense held its own, but a suddenly sputtering offense doomed the team to a 6–10 finish. Disappointed with the team's lack of progress, Baltimore fired Ted Marchibroda as head coach.

THE RAVENS' POINT-SCORING woes in 1998 led them to look for an offense-minded coach to replace Marchibroda. After interviewing several prospects, Baltimore chose Minnesota Vikings offensive coordinator Brian Billick to be the team's new head man.

During five years with the Vikings, Billick had put together one of the most fearsome offenses the NFL had ever seen. During the 1998 season, Minnesota scored an NFL-record 556 points, with 38 of those points coming in a 38–28 victory over the Ravens. The impressive offensive showing opened the eyes of the Baltimore front office. "We had identified Brian as one of the top young coaches in the game," said Ravens owner Art Modell. "But after that performance, we became convinced that he would be our top choice."

Λ

Billick surveyed his roster and saw a lopsided team. His rising defense was already among the best in the league. With the great linebacking trio of Lewis, Boulware, and Sharper, and with other standouts such as Siragusa, Woodson, ends Rob Burnett and Michael McCrary, and talented young cornerbacks Duane Starks and Chris McAlister, the Ravens could put a stranglehold on opposing offenses. But with the exception of Ogden, Baltimore's offense had just mediocre talent.

Billick was known for his love of a strong passing game. In Baltimore, though, he realized he didn't have the type of talent needed to run a high-scoring, passing offense. Instead, he installed a low-risk, run-oriented offense, choosing to rely on the strength of the rugged Ravens defense.

In 1999, the Ravens stumbled to a 3–6 start. But in the middle of the season, the team took off. The offense sprang to life, averaging 26 points per game the rest of the season. Much of the offensive spark came from quarterback Tony Banks and receiver Qadry Ismail. Banks stepped in at mid-season and tossed 17 touchdown passes, while the speedy Ismail posted more than 1,000 receiving yards. Behind these efforts, Baltimore won five of its last seven games to finish 8–8. "We've built a little fire here," said Coach Billick. "It will be interesting to see how big it gets."

DESPITE THE HOT finish to the 1999 season, Billick knew his offense needed more punch. So, in the first round of the 2000 NFL Draft, Baltimore selected bruising running back Jamal Lewis from the University of Tennessee. The 5-foot-11 and 230-pound Lewis gave the Ravens the big, powerful runner they needed.

The Ravens also added offensive firepower by signing veteran tight end Shannon Sharpe and quarterback Trent Dilfer. Sharpe, a seven-time Pro-Bowler while with the Denver Broncos, gave the Ravens a reliable target who could still make the big play. Dilfer, a former starter with the Tampa Bay Buccaneers, was signed to serve as Banks's backup.

The Ravens got off to a quick 5–1 start in 2000. Baltimore's defense led the way, not allowing a single point in three of those six games. But oddly, the Ravens offense, which had looked so promising at the end of the previous season, got worse in 2000. Banks struggled with interceptions, fumbles, and inaccuracy as the Ravens went an amazing five straight games without scoring an offensive touchdown.

Looking for an offensive spark and fewer mistakes, Coach Billick started Dilfer at quarterback in the season's second half. The decision proved to be a good one as Dilfer led the Ravens to seven straight victories to end the season. Ray Lewis and the defense again paved the way, giving up only 165 total points (an NFL record for a 16-game season). The great defense—coupled with Dilfer's solid passing and Jamal Lewis's 1,364 rushing yards—carried the Ravens to a 12–4 record and their first playoff appearance. "We're no offensive juggernaut," said Sharpe. "But we don't have to be. If we score 17 points, Ray [Lewis] and the 'D' will make it stick."

In the playoffs, the Ravens proved Sharpe correct, beating the Denver Broncos, Tennessee Titans, and Oakland Raiders while allowing only 16 total points. In the Super Bowl, Baltimore faced a tough New York Giants team. But the Ravens could not be stopped. Dilfer hit receiver Brandon Stokley with a touchdown pass, and swift receiver Jermaine Lewis returned a kickoff 83 yards for another score as Baltimore rolled to a 34–7 victory. After the game, team owner Art Modell was presented the Super Bowl trophy. "To the people of Baltimore and the state of Maryland, this belongs to you," he said with tears in his eyes. "From the bottom of my heart, thank you."

BEFORE THE START of the 2001 season, the Ravens made a change at quarterback, bringing in former Kansas City Chiefs quarterback Elvis Grbac and releasing Dilfer. Grbac was considered a more polished passer than Dilfer, and Baltimore hoped he would add life to the Ravens' low-scoring offense. The Ravens' hopes were dealt a serious blow, however, when Jamal Lewis suffered a season-ending knee injury during training camp. "Jamal is our bread and butter," said guard Edwin Mulitalo. "The rest of us will have to step it up."

Despite the loss of Lewis, the Ravens put together a strong 10–6 season and qualified for the playoffs. Hopes ran high after Baltimore beat the Miami Dolphins 20–3 in a first-round showdown but disappeared the next week in a 27–10 loss to the Pittsburgh Steelers.

After the loss, Baltimore let Sharpe and Woodson leave town as free agents, choosing to give young tight end Todd Heap and safety Ed Reed starting roles. Baltimore hoped the youth movement would energize the team, but unfortunately, the Ravens' bad luck with injuries continued. Defensive leader Ray Lewis suffered a shoulder injury that kept him off the field most of the 2002 season. The Ravens' quarterback situation also took an unexpected turn when Grbac retired before the season, leaving veteran Jeff Blake and youngster Chris Redman to run the offense. Despite strong showings by Heap, Reed, and a healthy Jamal Lewis, the 2002 Ravens went just 7–9.

Baltimore approached the 2003 season looking to add more young talent. In the 2003 NFL Draft, the team used its first-round picks on pass-rushing linebacker Terrell Suggs and quarterback Kyle Boller. Suggs, who had set a college record with 24 quarterback sacks during his final season at Arizona State University, was expected to make the defense even stronger. Boller, meanwhile, was named the team's starting quarterback as a rookie and looked to lead the Ravens offense for years to come. Both players contributed immediately as the 2003 Ravens captured the AFC North Division and returned to the playoffs with a 10–6 mark.

Since settling in Baltimore, the Ravens have taken their fans on a thrilling rollercoaster ride—a ride that has included both last-place lows and world championship highs. As Baltimore's football-crazy fans continue to root for their adopted heroes, the day may soon come when the Ravens once again fly high over the rest of the NFL.

INDEX>